The Man Who Spoke To Owls

Also by David H W Grubb

Prose:
Beneath the Visiting Moon
The Almost Child
Sorry Days Are Over
Sanctuary

Poetry:
The Green Dancers
The Burial Tree
And Suddenly This
From the White Room
Somewhere There Are Trains
Falconer
Last Days of the Eagle
Mornings of Snow
Figures and Masks
The Mind and Dying of Mr Punch
Stone Moon Poems
Return to the Abode of Love
Replies For My Quaker Ancestors
Three Meeting Houses
Village Poems
A Banquet for Rousseau
Romanian Round
The All Night Orchestra
The Rain Children
Turtle Mythologies
Bosnia
Dancing with Bruno
A Country Alphabet
An Alphabet of Light
Conversations Before the End of Time
The Man Who Thought He Was
The Memory of Rooms
The Elephant in the Room
Out of the Marvellous
It Comes With a Bit of Song

As Editor:
The Gifted Child at School
An Idea of Bosnia
Sounding Heaven and Earth

The Man Who Spoke To Owls

DAVID H W GRUBB

Shearsman Books
Exeter

Published in the United Kingdom in 2009 by
Shearsman Books Ltd
58 Velwell Road
Exeter EX4 4LD

www.shearsman.com

ISBN 978-1-84861-047-7
First Edition

Acknowledgements

Some of these poems previously appeared in the following:
*Ambit, Poetry Salzburg Review, The Journal, Poetry Review, Shadowtrain, Stride,
With, Iota, Strokestown Competition, English Association, Biscuit, Ragged Raven,
Kent and Sussex Competition, Neon Highway, Geometer, Oversteps, Troubadour,
Sign, The Matthew's House Project.*

CONTENTS

Part 1

Part 2

Part 3

for Beverly

PART 1

Intro

Before you read this book you need to be aware
that everything that has been said before by
Helen Joyce Bellbarker
is cancelled.

When we read the manuscript it had been with
an agent for three years and when he died
his wife used chapter one as wallpaper
she told us.

The opening scenes about parrots and the meaning
of rain are better set aside or perhaps used as opera
but it is a fact that windscreen wipers, laser printers
and bullet-proof vests were all invented by women.

11 of the 12 men who have walked on the moon
were in the Boy Scouts so they were used to rules
and rituals and nonsense and places where others
did not want to go.

Meanwhile Helen is training to become a monk
and all of her dresses are to be sold and the book
is about to be published by Invisible Press
who once published comics.

Isaac Newton invented the cat flap and there are two
chapters in the book about zoos in modern wars where
the animals moved out and the homeless moved in
converting cages etc.

There is also a chapter about etc and things that be
in dreams and the socks of Wallace Stevens and
why writing wrecks routine.

A House with No Windows

1.
They will all be talking at once and the words will tumble
so much that the grandfather will stand up on his chair
screaming for them to stop.

2.
There will be a very long silence and perhaps some conversation
about nuns blowing up balloons or the child who underwent an
operation and came out of it well but with a foreign accent.
(Laughter)

3.
There will be no conversation about the war.

4.
Who is it that has come to live at 55 and will they throw a party?
The last people who lived there; details and rumours and too many dogs.

5.
There is talk of a dead child found in a shed.
(Silence)

6.
Spunk. How can that be spoken without giving offence? Now that the
bishop has shaved off his beard are we to expect other things?

7.
Throughout these chapters everything speeds up and most of the
speakers actually sing.
(Is this to become an opera?)

8.
Some talk of poetry and Dunster at dawn and the idea of a house with
no windows. What to do with a gardener who is going mad and making
tea for the tulip tree.

9.
The carol singers have gone on strike. All the main speakers who have been singing now take to their violins so this cannot be an opera really. Each chapter will end with a birth and a house with no windows.

10.
They do not know what to do about the war? They do not like drums. They are very different people in winter. He is also writing about lichen.

Waiting For The Angels

Annie

I do not like the silent rooms. I do not like the way
the air is filled with hair and angels.
I do not like the silent rooms. I do not like the sideways
of their words and what the doctors mumble to each other
and the ramblings of their obsessions and the way it is never
dark enough to dream and look what the man in white brought in!
What is the point of a baby here? Dear God; the baby has been broken
and all I have is a doll who does its thing on my lap and I give it hymns.
Today is God Day again. I do not like the God Day because I like the God
who does not snore, who does not smile, who sits in his alone and never
        winks
and never asks for me to do that thing and sometimes his face is more
        like rain.
Monday is taps. All day the baths are filled and we swim like swine and
        the stuff
gets in our gobs and the drying takes us into freezing and all I can do is
        running so
fast I sometimes drop my face on the floor and hope that mother will come
        and pick
it up and stick it on again and I wonder a bit what she sees when there is
        no face.

Bill

Don't do it when they ask me anymore. Don't play music. Forget all tunes.
        Forget
her singing and the skipping songs and what the teacher said about a tune
        for every
truth. Sit at the piano now, in the small room now, in the old part of the
        house now,
and sometimes speak to the keyboard which is a beautiful thing. The
        waiting notes.
The expectations. The beautiful thing.

13

Mary

The Blue Angel comes on Mondays. Her eyes are rain.
The Green Angel arrives on Tuesdays. Only sometimes she does not come.
The Red Angel enters on Wednesdays, always at twelve o'clock. She
holds a bag full of nails.
The Yellow Angel crash lands on Thursdays. Then he runs on the spot.
The Brown Angel never turns up.
The White Angel is blind. Coming or going or what?
The Black Angel plays a kazoo. I think he can do tricks.
There are no angels on Saturdays and on Sundays we do not need them.
On Sundays we sometimes dress in wings and scare the pants off the others
or we get inside some words and don't come out.

William

I keep getting back to the farm. Every day I smell it.
I can see right through the hills to the back door and the pram.
I can hear her and the kids and sometimes the pigs.
It takes a long time for me to get out from under all these dreams
and I suppose I need proper clothes and proper words
but I can't do that because of the earth.

Margaret

Quiet as quilt
Silent as egg
Naughty as nettle
Crisp as cabbage
Secret as silence
Seldom as sorry
Hard as pardon
Waiting as water
Eager as earth
Mother as bell
Doctor as bum

Nurse as worse
Baby as midnight
God as glass

Tim

I write these letters you see. I write them every.
I catch the sound and ground it down and sentence it.
I have a way with that and what you need to understand
is that there is no need for more than rhyme
for you all remember rhyme and rhyme will not
and what goes up stays up; whatever is said stays said.

Melba

Please tell me something nothing
will also do so long as you tell me
using words not dead birds and even
carrots would be nice to hear them
snap and crack like fingers in case
nothing ever comes here again; again.

Archie

Where do they put the dead angels, after
they have crash landed in some field?
Or do they send them here, one or two,
dressed in light and kindness and sometimes
unseen in the snow; sometimes hiding in the
empty flower vase above the broken television?
I expect that's it.

THE COLOUR OF ANGELS

1.

It depends on the time of day, wind tides,
what we have not been saying, in which case
it is the brown angel, bark dark with slats of green
and eyes like an early autumn morning, head down
as if looking for something on the ground, a thing
that might be missed, something that will be crushed
beneath and remain there all winter, as if a lost message.

2.

Whereas the blue angel can be heard rushing about
as if it should be busy at a miracle or ready to carry
off a dead baby or at the place of a conversation when
the bully takes pity or the lunatic says something that
is so beautiful it shines and everyone falls silent; more,
more, you only need to say more and we will adore you
and forgive you all the years of silence and upsidedown.

3.

The white angel is always there. Of course you cannot
see him as he opens a door or a window or tips a book
onto the floor. The white angel scribbles messages on
the lake and sometimes he claps his hands at midnight
and you wake up and check the house for burglars or
in the midst of the radio announcement there is a long
buzzing and when it is over you feel like a stranger.

4.

Wait. The red angel always arrives about now. He has
a box of lies for you to choose from. He has a sack of

excuses and get out clauses and revels in denials. If you
ask him what truth is he laughs so much he begins to fart
and the veins in his head wriggle like worms and his hands
get the jitters. So do not do this. Let him come and go and
never pick up what he leaves on the table. Let it bleed dry.

5.

The pink angel of course you enjoy. The pink angel looks
a bundle of fun, ready for a dance, a polka, a prance and all
that jazz. The pink angel has a box of chocolates for each
one of us and wants to meet the children and wake up the
dead and throw a party for the nuns and what about a swim
at dawn? Only it is too late. The war has only just begun.
The pink angel will have to wait, take up yoga, get a real job.

6.

When it is time for the green angel to arrive there will be
a slight drop in the temperature of the field, the tennis court,
the lane, the hedgerow. The horses will know it and the birds
will all rise and fall again in seconds as a sign. There will be
no words. The angel will be there to remind us of the way all
things are changing, how the visible hides things, how a silence
has its story, how sunshine and moonglow may not return. Ever.

7.

That summer, when the drought bit the land raw, we all knew
that the chapel would rise from the lake again, crusted white and
gold, and that some would want to pray there and recall the names;
and there would be the dead to look after and even ghosts; and we
sensed that there were angels there, entwined, holding hands; and some
said they had seen them with their children of light and that they wore
robes of every shade, shafts of colour, as if they were dressed in music.

ANGELS

There is this distance. Not that I mind. It sometimes comes
when late afternoon meanders towards early evening and
the cows are lying down looking like earnest academics.
Then comes the thrush busy letting you know about worms
and survival and people are entering their gardens in case
nature is leaving them behind again after light rain. This is
when angels come or the idea of messengers or there is an
expectation that what has been said has more than ordinary
significance and there is this distance and we are not ready.
Three red kites fly over our neighbour's house as if the idea
of tomorrow did not exist, was not necessary. Wings of pale
fire as they circle within the essence of their being above us.
Then come the evenings when we think of earth and moths
and how the moon seems to visit our very own gardens and
how the same voices come back to us telling the same stories
although with different endings and the mood of our beings
appears also transformed because there is less time or even
too much time and our gods appear to be changing their songs
and masks and most certainly the language of love has changed.
What all this is about is part of the journey, the geography and
terrain and language and the map we have carried in our heads,
What all this is about is deaths and weddings and old books
and barbed wire dreams and the expectation of self and what
we inherit. Not that I mind. Not that the distance trembles.
Not that the voices are here to deny what the night may bring.
The fields at the edge of the town gently bending in the wind
that is silent and the movement like thousands of angels who
prepare for births and betrayals and the next child of light.

FIRE SERMONS FOR JAMES AGEE AND WALKER EVANS

Sunlight against the door like a stricken angel;
what is this for but to remind us that America is not
interested in poverty, places where nothing happens,
days that contain hours and nothing else?
This is where the poor speak slowly in case they
are to be regarded as idiots; the words do not do
when they get you nothing in return and the poor are
players in a romance that can be fixed later when wars
have been won and stories can sell books and there is even
the film of poverty that is about yearning and retreat and the
ability to spell it out against rain and high skies and the noble
bishop who distributes words that can be worn on a Sunday.
So you hold the camera still and capture these masks, you meet
people who have sold their dreams and the children, they cannot
even gather weeds to give to you. Neither can they sing or dance and when
you ask them about the days ahead they, and when you ask them about
games they, and when you ask them about future there is this quiet look in
their eyes that is a tale of terror. So this is reported, this is
made into prayers and poems, this is a narrative of earth angels and the
death of dreams and the words that are spoken to a wall at night when
looking at stars is pointless and the school bus has already left and any
bird in the sky may be a spy or a sign and Sunday is the only day when
you may recognize angels or yourself or the ghost that you have hold of
and when sleep gives you another story or screams or books without words.
For there is no way out, this is the story, this is the blessing, the
earth and rain and the deaths of small creatures and the shape of an angel
who has somehow crashed into the door; sign, warning, nothing;
the God passing over because your words are bone and stone and the God
needs trumpets and horses of fire and chambers of the naked who
have no other home but who have put this down in diaries and letters
and testaments and stories and images that search us beyond dreams.

CHRISTOPHER SMART'S FLOWERS AND HARDSHIPS

> for flowers are peculiarly
> the poetry of Christ

1

Christ comes down with tulips in His hair
        as words are worlds
           and what I see

       Oh it is true

       gathers

    across our lives
       to become

       God's witness.

2

Christ comes down in apple days
      as words are worlds
       that between virtue

       and it is true

       and acceptance

     the prayer
      is radiant

       within us.

3

Christ comes down and grass is silence   and we hear
                the words of longing
                        and converse

                                              with angels now

                arum lilies
                        between here

                                              and somewhere.

4

For flowers are peculiarly the poetry of Christ   coming
                into our lives
                radiant and expecting

                                              they abide in light

                and then
                        become

                                              another thing

the music
of
amens.

5

And there are days when only darkness dances
and I do not see Him in the sun
and words gather their accusing fingers
and HARDSHIPS catch me out
between a here and there
and I am blind before a mirror:

the HARDSHIP of bent sleep
the HARDSHIP of the Watchman spying
the HARDSHIP of wearing rain
the HARDSHIP of stuck song
the HARDSHIP of fled flowers
the HARDSHIP of a cat murdered
the HARDSHIP of a broken eye
the HARDSHIP of ideas that leap
the HARDSHIP of the angel that bites
the HARDSHIP of fools dancing
the HARDSHIP of nails in the head
the HARDSHIP of comforting ghosts:

but I am up early

                    I am   racing
                                                             with faith

I am running in His majesty

                                                    and Jesus is here

in this grass and this rain and this sunrise

and all such glories

shall burst

upon us

ever

EMILY DICKINSON AND THE SNOW DAYS

Sometimes it is so cold it makes me think of whales
and their seeking songs
and the way that every tree is keeping birds alive at night.

There are few visitors and their messages are brief
and they must be gone
even before they have finished speaking.

The small garden has become a white lake
and if there were anybody walking there
they would surely whisper

in case a story escaped or something they had not wished
and nothing would ever be the same
or it would be hidden in a poem.

When the snow goes there will be several of these poems
placed about the house
as if to reach an understanding

or I will pass one down and know that there are people
hearing my voice in their heads
and folding the paper over and over

as if between the lines and rhymes
and the invisibility of each page
something must fly.

EMILY DICKINSON AND THE WORDS AGAIN

She enters the upstairs room and somebody has again
thrown words all over the bed, the desk, the floor, the mirror,
the upright chair, the fingernail, the place where there should be
a vase of flowers, the drapes, the pile of *Playboy* magazines;

so who is this who enters her world and makes her pick up
each word and place it in a perfection and exploit the sound
and why do they never introduce themselves and come to the
front door and proclaim their identity and purpose and tell her
that they love her even more than cowboy movies etc?

She never tells anybody about this. She never writes poems
about this which is odd because don't you think this might
make a good poem or short story or even a ballet? The dancer
with words to scatter. The secret visitor who spreads letters
that will become words that will become sentences that will
change the meaning of life for everyone who reads them and
get them to give up robbing banks or attempting to grow roses
or those who sit in small silent libraries waiting for the book
babble to begin revealing what poetry and death are here to do.

EMILY DICKINSON'S JOKE BOOK

In the upstairs room
where snow could be seen but not heard,
where downstairs voices stopped at the front door,
where the window watched for tricks of light,
Emily also worked on her *Book of Jokes*;
about answers without questions,
about the way words made silences,
about the collapse of impulses,
about the arrival of strangers,
about where an idea went when she didn't use it,
about the determination of the garden,
about visitors from England,
about the silences in dreams;
about what other people said that she meant
in some poems that appeared to have a voice
of their own;
about how errors corrected conformities,
about the seconds when an afternoon becomes an evening,
about how we can seldom tell who we will never meet again,
about the way we dress for dances and deaths,
about what is lost between stopping and the starting of a clock;
about how we all go into the sky to die.

EMILY DICKINSON AND THE MEANING OF SNOW

When the snow arrives
there is this interval to
understand between
what is given and what
we understand of nature
and the meaning we give
to the things we accept
and the anticipation
of the new in the window
in the garden in the letters
from people we do not know
and the birds that give us
the originality of the old
as if what we hear has never
been sung before.

The Man Who Spoke to Owls

He was good at this. He did not ask any questions.
He did not expect them to invent proverbs.

They came in the early evening, flying between silent
boughs, experts in identifying.

Sometimes the man stood at the field's edge speaking
out loud as if to a dog or child,

talking about his garden, nesting, the moles returning
and what the wind had done.

He was good at this. He did not attempt anything
elaborate. He simply stored these things.

When he died there was nobody to tell the owls
and so for them his voice remained.

They liked the way he repeated things.

EVERY SILENCE

Every silence has its own noise,
every noise has its own silence;
every vision has its blind spot,
every blind spot has its revenge;
every word has its own meaning,
every meaning has its variations;
every gardener has his winter,
every winter has its stars;
every prayer has its desire,
every desire has its lost room;
every dance has its narrative,
every narrative has its ending.

Every silence has its own gardener,
every gardener has his own noise;
every revenge has its own narrative,
every narrative has its winter;
every dance had its desire,
every desire has its blind spot;
every variation has its ending,
every ending has its lost room;
every star has its dance,
every dance has its noise;
every prayer has its vision,
every meaning has its own word.

HER LIGHT

The bees are aware that she is vibrant again;
each time she speaks to them at the hive they know
that her heart is filled with stories that have no endings
and her light has yet to discover its passages and windows.

The bees wait for her each day now, her flowers and meadows,
her earth and streams, and at night they know that she is
dreaming beyond love and expectation.

They wait for her story to end;
they know that the man will come to tell them;
this knowledge is like a wind without an end; each word
that he brings informing them that she has already
entered another field.

IN THE AMERICAN NIGHT

for Richard Wilbur

In the American night, something that slips between
childhood and stories of war and old light.
Each day men come to remove the trees and change
the names of buildings
and at the Walt Whitman Service Station
there isn't much time for words.
What will come will come and time plays tricks
says the wind sitting in the park waiting for dawn
and somewhere in this ocean of dreams and impulse
there are the poets who do not wait for madness, who
have all night found their minds wrapped in grass and
wings and the voices of their teachers telling them how
a story can be laid down in the soul for years before it
reveals its truth, its necessity, its refusal and ballyhoo.
What will the words do now, the tunes quite changed,
the way we make our meanings on the screen and the
key board is the only sound? Scroll. Lock. Page Up.
Page down. Delete. And print the meaning so that
it means to those who cannot be here. Where do they
hide? Somewhere between Home and End; good night.

IN THE CITY THAT DOES NOT EXIST

In the city that does not exist we all meet,
to talk, to walk, to hear the cathedral bells
and see women with prams and enormous babies
and beggars who smoke cigars and there are policemen
with umbrellas and in the cafes men waiting for mothers;

and it is deliberate the way the music is played and
it is accidental the way that windows fall out and when
we bump into friends we leave it to other people to pick
them up and apologise for the state of the pavements and litter
and why is the park plagued by all this broken glass?

And there is Gogol again, he who makes stories, he who has
met God and talked to Him and known His ambience, he who
might wear a bright tie and describe the true nature of angels,
who sits at the small table and consumes the cheapest soup
looking for all the world as if he has never tasted reality;

how many stories will he take to his grave with him, what will
he do in Heaven to occupy eternity, what shall we say about him
in this city that does not exist with paper poets and songs that are
so easily forgotten and the man with the mouth-organ grin telling
us that we must vote for him and the sound of the silent birds?

Over there they continue to dig up the bodies of children and
the museum now has a resident dancer who stands quite still
and waits for old men to ask her for a quick one; and the big
idea from the publishing world is the Book of Blank Pages
where you write your own lies and give the book to a stranger.

Indiana Jones and the Kingdom of Necessity

I no longer hear from my father. He is possibly writing
the final draft of A Short History of something or other.
It could be bagpipes or umbrellas. When he's good and
ready I'll hear from him at length and my students will
ask me why I look so demented. Meanwhile there's a
strange woman who keeps emailing about the fifty two
angels of Abrahonna and do I want to know more and
did I know that when the bees die out we all have four
years left? Quaint. She has started sending me samples.
Wings and accounts of visitations and remnants of maps
of the palaces and fortifications and the only remaining
copy of The Wisdoms. There is apparently a man in the
west of Scotland who specialises in angel rants and at
any moment she will send me his attempts to unravel
the tongue and truths and preoccupations of the angels
of Abrahonna or it might be Abrahinna or even Abrax.
Perhaps if I get my father to speak to the man in the
windy wilds that will put a stop to it. Perhaps my father
had better meet this woman. Perhaps all three of them
can be persuaded to make a trip to Abrahonna and the
angels will enchant them or eat them and I can get back
to doing absolutely nothing; no adventure, no discoveries,
no trails or trials or women who have secret skins. And
then there is this mad poet who keeps sending me stuff
from Blake. What was he on? Poems and pictures and
there's a box of letters on the way. So; why fifty two?
Were there more? And why Wisdoms? Why bees?

Inventions at the Asylum

We can do running and throwing light and watch out
for the angels of upsidedown and trees they fall over
and the quiet is a dance without shadows
between what we see and what we settle for
and the chairs that are blue to begin with.

The chairs are blue to begin with and there is my father
tapping out words and sermons and the bits between what
may make a hymn and a howl and a do never know
and here it is that he sits in the blue of the thing and
the woman is my mother with white silence.

The woman is my mother with white silence
that used to be songs and apple sized riddles and there
were always children in the trees and a small doorway
for the spiders and woodlice and one winter a rat
and the old lady who lived upstairs in the sky.

The old lady who lived upstairs in the sky
knew that the dust would return early every morning
and that is why women arrived to clean and tidy and set
about order which was also about the way words came out
and certain things were to be hidden from the daylight.

The certain things were sex that would drive you mad and
gangsters who could never be seen as their cars cruised past
and the people who worked at the nightmare factory and
experimented on animals and pushed the angels over in small
countries where there was nothing to go in the windows.

There was nothing to go. It was like being under snow.

Mr and Mrs B Entering Heaven

All the way from Derbyshire with their six grandfather clocks
all telling a different time and all transformed now because
there was no time to tell;

and there was no need for spectacles or hot water bottles or books
and the big bed that was somehow more like a ship of whispers
and things still unsaid;

and whatever would the radio be saying without them as they
gradually moved forward looking for people
they might have known?

Quiet as quilt, as pillow;
as slippers, as unmade.

There was no place for dreams
and Mr B gave up calling Mrs B his Little Angel
because everyone had wings;

and what they saw or thought they saw melded into mosaic,
and faces faced them back like little lanterns
and the voices sounded like grass;

and they knew it would take some time (only time did not exist),
they would gradually grow accustomed to living here (although
there was no living to be done); no trees, no windows, no roses;
silent as light, as spent; as ever, as told;

and the clocks, wound down, with nothing to do,
were used by the hide and seeking children of Heaven
who waited to be born again.

Peace Musick

1.

A quiet peace of music
is making its way up the valley

and the woman smiles as she hangs
the fish up to dry

and the man who prepares a hole
in the earth whispers a smile

and the teacher tells the class that
the last thing they may hear is trees

screaming and hills saying "told you
so" and somebody will let out lions

and we will all listen to RADIO TEN
in case there is still hope and messages

but for now the future is rubbish and
the rain decides not to and music is

and what they will do with dreams is
another thing you must never ever do.

2.

We were dancing when they said it
&
we were singing when they said it must go
&
the trumpet played as they left us

&
and I heard organ music as they fled
&
a boy was blowing grassblade when they caught them
&
an owl flew across when the doors were locked
&
the music man came each week
&
cycled away when we had come alive.

3.

When it snows
I call across fields
to see what comes next
and it is often John Clare
who hears
and puts it
into
words.

4.

Cannot fix it in words any more
but that's where music comes in
and the man at the piano
tells me that he is called Scarlatti
and I believe him
even when it never quite ends.

PEOPLE FROM PORLOCK

People from Porlock usually arrive when an egg has gently fallen or the dog has got caught in the log pile or the rain has found a way under the garage door just where the antiquarian books have been temporarily stored or the box of early drafts of the novel that keeps changing its name but there is always the word Great in the title as if it all depended on sudden horizons and discovered love or a room with several doors all of them leading to the entrances of dead friends.

People from Porlock are actually more likely to come from Padstow or Penzance escaping from the stones and picture post cards and roads that come back on you and tracks to farms that are stranded in winter and where just when you thought there might be a café there appears to be another church surrounded by white grass and split gravestones and there are voices of people passing by on their way to a beginning that waits along a lane and across to a hunch of cottages with no names.

People from Porlock have a lot to say about silences and dead owls and the way October gets into their beds and gives them babies and some will want to make observations about letters never sent and how there are often other voices on the telephone line telling them about events that should remain private and meetings in the library and about the books that arrive in the post with missing pages which adds to the idea that it is the reader who is really in charge making every word unique.

People from Porlock never let on how long they might stay as they let you into the lost lanes of their existence and surmise what the year will bring to us all between the constant turning off of televisions and the places never heard of and the things that can be seen behind bent curtains and the way that folk still remember the faces at windows as the postperson arrives with a letter from Chicago or Belfast or Berlin telling a story of another world that may or may not actually exist.

People from Porlock depart leaving us where we were to pick up the egg and send for the vet and rearrange the garage and return to the poem that was evolving and decipher the meanings of what was said and wonder at the names of winds and the sudden closing of doors and the sight of a woman pushing a bike across the moor and what was the name of the man who spent years building a drive to his front door and how it was used for the first time on the day they came to bury him?

Remembering to Forget

There is nobody at the front door
so who is it she is answering to?
There is nobody in the small garden
but she needs to stop them stealing.
The telephone is silent but she waits
to hear what it has to say and soon
she will get up and make it some tea,
and when she smooths, smooths, strokes
her hands it is as if she had been hiding
a prayer or something to give her dead
husband whose old raincoat still hangs
in the hall as if we might have hidden
him in another story, in case the wind
gets in or the trees want more, in case
she hears the voice of a child again;
"never, never, never."

THE HORSE WITH ONE EYE

What is it you are meant to say when they look the other way
as if this still beautiful creature now had half a mind
or they want precise details and do we think the horse
still sees in its dreams?

We tell them we are still waiting to hear from the Horse Dream Doctor
and that he will one day come and speak to the horse,
meanwhile the old eye is kept in a small and very ornate box
specially made by a local cabinet maker
and that the person who did this terrible thing is known.

The photographer could still see light in the horse's mind
and in the way it held its head;
not to be ruined, never to yield to a memory of pain and broken moon
and the way the man ran in a tangle down the valley
as if his demons had turned on him.

The Horse Dream Doctor came in snow and rain
and on the days when the sky was high he rode him
through a valley and fields that nobody else could see.

Passing Wonderful

I want to tell the man who is in charge of the red parrots
about the green parrots and the yellow ones and the white ones;
I want to advise the man who sweeps the streets outside the big hotel
to enter the desert and take his duster to the dunes at dawn;
I want to ask the people who write the speeches for the great ones
to go away and read the silent letters of the dead;
I want to suggest to the gardeners in the public parks that they visit
the fields of stones and the avenues of broken roses;
I want to propose to the nuns who are looking up at the sun
that they climb into the chambers of the earth to find ancient children;
I want to lead the sniper to the place where he can be sure to kill
his mother and his father and his wife before he goes away to eat;
I want to ask the priest what it is that he hears at the back of his head
and where all his stories are born as he slips between visions;
I want to show the old man with a horse in his head where it is
that the blue dogs sleep and their blue puppies are born;
I want to listen to the beautiful children who sometimes tell us
that there are certain stories than cannot ever be told
and about the wind that they will hear when their grandfathers die
and about the wonders that wait at the centre of each winter field.

THE SOUND OF A SHORT STORY

A window is opening into rain,
a letter slowly falls in shreds,
barbed wire sings at the fields's edge,
the clergyman mutters as he grabs the spider;
her boy is blowing on a blade of grass,
a crow greets the yellow balloon,
ice enters the farmer's dreams again;
the church clock times us all,
a girl calls "Ruby, Ruby, come home."

The World at Last a Meadow

Gerald Stern

So when we are writing about our lives
there can suddenly be this recognition
so that we understand our fathers dancing in rain
and our mothers holding the stories in their arms
as if we might break them, the trust in them, and get
to other places that are off the map, beyond beyond,
and yet there are connections: the names of birds and
heart songs and islands in the mind and the rasp of whispers
and the way we connect with gangsters and bishops and the
boy Christ playing with miracles, and especially the memory
of hotels where everyone we have ever known has stayed before
and we sleep in the midst of other people's dreams and perhaps
we are ahead of their dreams because we have already visited the
gardens and seen the roses that are hidden in grasses and we have noted
the tennis courts buzzing with muscle before the games have even set
fire, and there has been this need to remind ourselves that this is all in
the mind and perhaps the soul is another place and what was love was
more about future and what we did not want to do about our futures.
And so there you have it; the meadow is about clowns and acrobats
and the tumbling time and what we let fall and the failure of dreams
and why it is that a beach or field or orchard never leave us and the
exact place and space where certain words were perhaps never said?

THINGS THAT CAN HAPPEN

for Vanessa

So, was it a pig we saw that sat at the piano
and was that Paul hunting for dead birds in the wood?
There was a man's voice for sure coming from the bottle;
meanwhile several fathers sat in their rooms of silence
attempting to hear the voice of God and the choirmaster
yet again told the boys what they must do to reach Top C.
There was a man searching for the tennis courts here;
he lost them about fifty years ago.
Who is it that keeps not coming back?
Things that can happen can often happen sideways.

PART 2

THE BEGINNING AND THE MUDDLE AND THE END

In the beginning was incontinence and distant voices and
the lapping of dreams in heads and beds and floating ghosts
and the world as it was between words and blitherings;

faces and noises and more words about the about and the way
the eyes spoke and escaping into tunnels of sleep and an awareness
of light and love and the way it all came together in a somehow;

then the muddle, the dislocations, the rebellion, the sexed up,
the other side, the other voices, every moment of every day as
the angel of distortions enters and calmly scrawls on walls;

and we never really recover; the music is seldom the same, what our
children say to us becomes another story in a world that is beyond
and we retreat to gardens and the idea of seasons and ornate abidings.

THE RAIN SENDS CHILDREN

Poem beginning with a line from Jeff Nuttall

The rain sends children whispering among the beech leaves;
they hide their hearts here and become other people
and the beech trees protect their savage secrets, their reaping
rebellions, the contortions of their lies.
In the land of their mud they discover pagodas of light,
broken flags, toys of fire, berries of passion, glass eggs,
severed wings and murals of lichen.
In the land of their blood they discover dance doctors
and watch a fornicating scarecrow, waterbomb rooks, run down
ladders, wait for the PIG MAN, speak to the great green unicorn,
decide who will live for ever, lose an eye.
In the land of their tribe the children whispering.
What would happen if the sky died?
The beech leaves answer in millions of traceries.
In the land of their soundings these silences with no names.

POEM FOR DAUGHTERS

For Emily and Clare

When you are not inventing games,
when you are not inventing names;
when you are not in that other world,
when the riddles will not do;
when skipping is for other kids,
when Doc Martin becomes dire;
when you tell us the names of things
and you inform us about the meaning of boys;
when you introduce us to the future,
when we get to know his name;
when the wedding day is here;
when I am expected to put this into words
there is this moment when I do not ever want to let you go;
and then I see that you are already flying
and I remember what this means
and the sunlight bursts upon your face.

My Father's Bells

1.

I did not trust my father's words;
they came out of a dark room spouting Latin,
declensions and what was never done and the drawer
where he kept his brother who had died on the rugger field.
He refused to sign the hospital forms before my operation;
a London hospital and Roman Catholic nurses, whereas if
it had been in Cornwall he could have buried me in wind.
His study confused me; drawers and cabinets and books that
nobody read and no music. The radio told us about Stalin and
God and children lost at sea. The room never smiled until Jaffa
Oranges phoned to say that he had won a prize; something he had
written about squeezing out the goodness of the sun. Ten lines.

2.

In Cornwall he wore his college tie in case he ran into
somebody from the past. We discovered his freckles and a scar
and were late for church each Sunday because we walked across
the cliff top and heard the Late Bell scolding. He never ever ran.
Seated in the pew with us he was lost. He could not find his god
and didn't even attempt the hymns. We did not bathe on Sundays.
We watched the others surfing and heard their laughter and wondered
if God liked the kites. What did He do on Sunday afternoons? When
the crowd has dispersed we walked on the beach and sometimes a van
arrived with a Jesus film. A small crowd gathered as the screen rolled
up and blotchy music prepared us for the big event. Moses was a Yank
and most of the people seemed to be in a hurry to die. It cost sixpence.

3.

Moon bite. My father stands on the lower lawn.
The fox has returned. My mother inspects what is left
but this is too much for him. It smashes the hymns in his head
and bells collide and the beauty of the world becomes stubborn.
What is it that the God believes? The hum in his head fracturing.
All night the dreams of the God Fox and rivers of eyes and what
was never said at the meal table and the careful construction of
stained glass prayers, waiting for the sun to let in truths and heart
riddles and threnodies of desire. In the corner of each prayer the
soft suggestion, the other truth, flesh fable and desire dancing
and shadow play exposing what we might become when the fox
and toys and mothers vanish and the silent moon enters the bed.

4.

Every word counts as memories collide and make up their own
history. What was it we saw in the orchard that forces us to return?
Standing at the porch my father waits for the procession to arrive;
the small coffin on a flower–filled wagon, the men uncomfortable
in suits, the women holding sunset's riddles and the bell calling for
grass dreams and memories and a life that they hold in their hearts.
And this is what he must proclaim for those who would believe in
angels and those who already dream of nettles. What are the words
meant to mean? Where are they taking us? The men do not dare look
him in the eye. In the earth all may be revealed as we face rain days
the stories become us and lichen writes what we wish to be told.
Each word cast on the field of the mind; memory, earth, silent light.

5.

The words become the silences
and the meadows where the games
took us away from things we could

not explain and the ways in which
so many things were denied and now
these are the bells in the head and the
moments we hid and the sounds that
we bury things in behind silence.

6.

We did not understand where your words
were coming from. In the pulpit, in the study,
in the garden, when you were speaking about
the sound of future and the voices of angels
and when the dog bit the postmistress you
were lost for words.

7.

Now that you are not here it is easier to speak
to you. I read your journals about visits to Ireland
and understand how you needed to escape and enter
fields of silence, stand with ancestors, the bells in your
head churning rain and rebellion and fidelities of blood.
You could never explain this. Each year it slipped further.
—Nettles. Lost orchards and the narratives of fallen walls.

8.

Sometimes you are there in an arrangement of words,
the ripple of a hymn, or coming across the lawn after a funeral
with whatever words could do, the contentments of light, these
agreements of faith. And now I would show you where we have
become, where we survive, what our words are saying as we greet
strangers and face down the howls, forgiving whispers and secrets
and embracing the linen fold truths of music and old expressions.

In Cornwall there are still tracks that rush towards the ocean and stones that circle winds and the sudden sight of places where they buried saints and whatever the rain was saying slanting towards us.

9.

What will these silences do in the forest of words, the seeking songs, the moments when memories collapse and we hold shattered hands? Each requiem, every violation, these torn testimonies and the sight of houses slipping into the sea;
wind bell, memory bell,
the never tell them bell,
silent sister bell, lost lawn bell,
hat box in the attic bell,
the bell that was buried in a suitcase in a dream that was meant to be forgotten because of what the voice might say about love and failure; in Italy in August the taxi took all morning to find the chapel that had nothing left but dead birds and the driver thought we were truly mad.

My Father Will Not Let Go

Early Easter morning and my father
has hallelujas in his head.
All night it has snowed and the driveway
is an encrusted robe as he sets out for the
church and those who have gathered
in a place of fragile expectations.
He is not the only one seeking something.
The Chinese geese would normally be looking
out for him by the side of the small lake; ornate
like emperors with their entourage emitting low
hoots, strutting beneath a white sun as if reminded
of a winter palace, ghost gardens, snow's precision.
Now they lie distorted, terror-dead, broken by the
fox who came earlier and made them mad; two
ice bound at the edge, the rest trapped in grass
and mud, blood stains rupturing their beauty.
My father halts in horror and then he carefully
stoops over each dead bird as if trying to find
words, something to say, the hint of a signal.
My mother enters the church and announces
that her husband will be late but they must begin
with an Easter hymn; they should celebrate, the
message is the same. The bells of heaven peal
and trumpets will enter their hearts. And they
rise and sing and bring back to life the words
they have known since they were children,
the ideas again rising beyond human wisdom
as father enters now carrying the massive form
of one of the dead birds in his arms, staring at
it as if it were the most valuable thing in the world,
to celebrate what it had been and the world it had
known and the dangers that we must all face and
the way that whatever happens there will be more.
And my father is also thinking of the fox, the way

it begins and finishes, its knowledge of killing, its flesh
territory and what it must have seen that morning as
the geese began their calls within a snow world, the
ritual movements of all creatures as they close in to kill,
the instinctive skill in a world beyond the human story.
The hymn is complete. The organ sighs it's amen. The
sounds of humans sitting down and waiting as my father
finds a place for the bird beside the Easter garden, laying
it down on moss, returning to the words that can never end.

* * *

All week my father could hear the fox entering snow.
No words. The trees had wings and the fox kept low.
Fox knowledge; fixed, rooted, informed by wind and
compulsion. Stars. The cut of clouds and the escaping
moon. And in some of his dreams my father heard
what the fox wanted to say about another planet where
the human did not exist and the nature of wild and where
all the rivers ran to. And there was the other god, the fox
god, the immense beauty of its ideas and culture and
harmony of laws and the way that water and wind
were maps, blood earth and bone being and earth without
end, without harm, without cruelty, without the human eye.

* * *

He will not let go of this. Snow melt. The bodies
of the other birds remaining by the lake and my mother
insisting that the bird in the Easter Garden be taken out.
My father has to decide to burn or bury them and let
the lakeside return to its normal state; the upturned
rowboat and the tall grasses and the moorhen run,

the ice giving way to the darkness of the water, the
way water waits in its natural chill, the silence of snails.
But he cannot let go of this. The fox will not yield and
my father stands on the small bridge caught in visions,
trapped by fox narratives and snow dreams and the event
of death, each bird taken by terror, the fox certainty,
the way a fox begins and finishes and then retreats
into places we do not know, cannot get to, the world
as another place, the mind of God alert to this, seeing.
And it is this that my father must work on, the way we
cannot pass into, the completeness of nature and void.
And when the flames take hold of the dead geese, the
wings, the eyes, my father is looking for other things;
tokens, stories that might explain, not holy things but
the dare of the ordinary, the ways we must survive, small
and necessary celebrations above and beneath the moon.

My father is looking for other things as we enter our
hiding times and other worlds where we hunt, adore,
meet people called Texas and Mister Shine and talk
to people who live in books and there is the man who
cannot get back to Poland because it is no longer there;
he shows us the creased image of his house and his field
and tells about the horses who were slaughtered by the
soldiers and the stolen things and how they ran from
that story into another story; eating stones, changing
names, the way that even the most ordinary memories
were now deep secrets. He told us where the silent
moorhen nest would be and that we must only look
at the eggs and that if we got too close the nest would
be deserted. The world would be changed for ever.
When we told my father this he got up from his desk
and stared out at the fields of Bedfordshire as if there
might be people there, other stories there, other lives.

Lux

1.

I was playing out behind the barn with God

Some say his voice is like oak but I'd call it moss

There must be times when he wants to sing

*

At the same time I could hear my father calling out to mother that the twins had died

The barn was the only place that the adults never thought of

It was September and the slugs had gone

*

Once I met a man who said he was me

Behind the barn we talked about why things had to die

God had the face of an owl and his body was rain

*

Once I met a boy who said he was me

You are the first person who has heard of this

If it had been January it would never have taken place

2.

What makes the poetry happen is sometimes a letting go

after the intensity of knowledge and feeling

and a desire to set down wonders

*

Each attempt creates a complexity of self

that has to be overcome which sometimes seems

like praying backwards

*

when all the time what one wanted was flow,

flight, song and the idea that provides something new,

a narrative that is determined and a discovery

*

Behind the barn you see fallen walls and log piles

Gates that had a purpose now lead nowhere

Silent crops and nettles

*

Snowbound it is a quilt of whispers

The sky sits on the stile

Dog bark to remind us

*

I asked God about nettles and dead babies

Sometimes the beautiful song is a warning

In spring the barn is always taller

3.

When I returned the barn was nowhere

There is sometimes a man in a field telling secrets

About lost children there is never an ending

*

The manner in which we have spoken to animals

Placing prayers in the spaces between ancient trees

Carefully closing the gates to ruins

FLYING IN THE FACE OF LOGIC

For Kier and Danny

The fruit fly looks just like my grandfather
about to tell us in a sermon about the meaning
of aboutness and the aboutness of meaning and
everything in between meaning and doubt and
the essentials of architecture in a barren landscape;
the eyes, the hood, the wisps of hair, the things that
appear to be coming out of the mouth that might just
be about how the planet will survive etc and dominations
and the way we share existence with invisible tribes;
so what are we to do in this clawback time, these buzzard
days when we see these creatures of the earth close up and
eyeball the tunes of territory and terror and begin to tell our
children about what was fox and badger and the buzz of bees?

MOUSEHOLE

i.m. Joan Gillchrest

What the sea says is not the same as fields,
water and rock, earth and stone have different voices;
rain days and weeks of wind pulling against
the harbour, gull yawp and crack of sudden gusts;
and when there is a lull the dogs keep their heads low
dragging their owners between these nests of stone,
and windows that watch and the woman who keeps
painting the sun green; leaps of light as if this village
might ring out with a bellow of ancient bells, in a shock
of sudden white; a snowman stares at the glass ocean.

THREE PRIESTS ON THEIR WAY

This one is bouncy and shaped like a bell;
his hair has been stolen by the birds to make their nests;
he is going to a civic dinner and has to make a speech
which means he will have to cut back on the wine;
he would like to tell them about the state of the roads
and why the hospital must never be closed but then
for years he has wanted to tell his one good joke;
he speeds up, he must not be late; will there be dancing?

This one has chosen to walk through the woods,
to embrace the view of daffodils, to approach the town
from the top so that he can see the steeples and towers
and flags and the flashes of sun on the river;
he has been asked to say The Grace and wonders
if Latin would be suitable, or something lighter about
fishes and dishes, or should he simply say Thank God?
He does not like the Mayor and his zipper grin.

This one wishes that he had not been invited;
perhaps there will be a sudden death and he will
be called away or one of the Chain Gang will fall
ill and he will be called to sit in the ambulance;
perhaps there will be a power failure and what
if one of the others were to fail to turn up; would
this mean that at last he could make his speech
about clowns, about the make up, about the tricks?

TUMBLE

WHAT'S IT LIKE
when the earth and stars
mix with the words and
sea gets in the memory
of being and seeing and
becoming something is
less of a proposition than
the preparation of being
as we all dance and drift
and the words are another
way forward and when is
it that we stop repeating
what we heard as children
and the skipping songs are
really the new psalms and
what was a conversation is
already a communion and
the angels become ghosts
and the promises are love
and rain is the memory we
walk with until we are at
last holding hands with a
person who may be father
or mother or the person we
were before this poem began?

WHAT WAS WILD

What was wild
was earth story and the way
wind ran across the grass
and all we remembered
is the way a field was
always somewhere else
with its seeds and other
time and birds and wind
and the visiting sky so
that when my father said
do not step on the crops
we thought he meant a
person sleeping or the
flowers of the future
or even those other
children who we heard
all the time and always.

WIND SONG

That he be not guilty of playing a game with meanings
and the ballyhoo of ways so that grass grows sideways
and we all become changed mirrors and what we meant
to be prayer has become ghost;

so go down quiet in the early hours and do not let the rain
endure and where there are roses run laughter and when a
boy appears with an eagle let the suddenness enshrine and
everything shall rise as if this were the first day of grass;

for we have a purpose here which is to be tremendous with
the words and let the avenues collapse and when they tell
us that this cannot hold we run towards the sun and let each
note of drum sound have its space to be present here and go
beyond the known so that these reasons will wild and tumble
and what we thought to be a wonder is no longer secret song.

When the Farm Was Breaking

When the farm was breaking she sometimes
walked down to the far field to see if the sea
was still there, searching for that line in the mind
where the eye latches sea and sky.

Returning to the house she felt that she had moved
from silver into grey and that the earth might hide
small abandoned things; candle ends, biscuit tins,
a doorknob or two, broken curtain rings.

In the kitchen she swore again because he had not mended
the tap, the larder window, and the pile of racing papers
might at any time topple over and bury her
in dead events.

But he was not here, even his soul had left the place
and now the wind visited and the huge elm tree rocked
as she went about her hours and dusted the grand piano
and carefully prepared food for the fox.

Each evening, after the fox had gone, she sat at the large
kitchen table waiting for her mother to speak and tell her
what was wrong and offer cures and then there was her brother
still bragging about diving off the cliff into a world of green;

and then, sometimes, there was that other voice and she knew
it was herself, wanting to know about nests and nettles and
where the skipping rope was hidden. The dead mother and
the dead brother perhaps would know.

WHERE WILL WE PUT THE WORDS?

Where will we put the words when we have finished our use of them?
There is no thing made for us to hide them in. They do not burn.
Silence is no answer. Our children will keep finding them
in old letters, diaries, greeting cards and instructions about clocks
and which key belongs to what.
Those who have written poems and stories have hidden riddles
and whispers in the folds of the future.
Even if finally the sentences fail us and we enter fiddle faddle
there will be something that pops out in good order, in another
wonder; the registration number of a car, the name of a lake,
the beginning of the beginning of a prayer.

QUESTIONS ABOUT HEAVEN

Does everybody die twice?
The first death is about body, the everyday,
the spit and polish living and the radio lies,
tokens and toenails and tidy lives.
The second death is about music and gardening
and wine, riddles and the memory of trees;
at least, I think this is so.
But then how can one be sure about anything
to do with Heaven?
Does God do jazz or opera, sunsets or B films?
Is this finally what it's all about;
the singularity of loss, the quality of distractions?
Does God do harp or kazoo?

WE ARE ALL GOING TO PAINT GOD

We are all going to paint GOD
we have done the words
and we have done the acrobats and now we will be all day painting
GOD
because HE is a very long field
and He comes and goes like snow
and HE shuts and opens like a gate
and when HE is asleep He sometimes looks like a swan
and HIS dreams are about poor boys and dancing girls and
men hurrying away from
and women wanting to hurry to
and the old who know that soon they shall be with HIM
in the park or by the lake or in the endless song or where
they have silence alltime long
and where love makes each word happy and nothing is hung down lost
and the painting that I shall make today
will have so much light in it
I expect I will have to take my glasses off and also my everyday mind
and even give up the whisting that I am so good at
they call me Songbird
and Nurse Williams will come and stroke me
and tell Doctor Williams
and he will tell the God Man
who comes once per week
with his little poems
and book of promises
and when he laughs his dentures shiver a bit
and I expect they will tell my children who at the moment sit at the edge
of the painting of God and have their backs to me and sometimes they
are also dressed in the sun
and there are some fish in the painting and men with bells and women
cutting a field of grass that turns into bread in their sturdy arms
and also the singing.

THE CLOSING

Coming back from nowhere sometimes takes longer
because we are carrying so many things and
the thermals confuse:
river   cloud   a silence   then voices   tracks

And what we said was more of a song that kept
coming and going like the lines in the last letter
from someone we loved:
don't forget   always ours   the things we know

And as we return there are secrets and stories
and things that surprise us, that don't latch,
that seem to belong to something else:
splinters   shadows   half a thing   loose

And in these moments there seems to be a trust and we
know that it will take longer and we are reminded
of other events almost lost:
a prayer line   a lost joke   her half smile   the closing.

THE BEAUTIFUL INTUITIONS

1.

A voice in the field calling autumn,
telling us that we have survived
stories, faiths, ourselves.

Leave some blackberries for the witches
and do you remember how we went into
the fields to kill the rabbits, sixpence a tail?

Once we arrived late for a funeral;
the wrong church, the wrong body,
the way the sermon died.

Flood time and these cathedrals like galleons
as sheep and dogs get stranded in trees
and some old folk refuse to leave.

A voice from outside in the night;
at three a.m. I try to write this down.
Was it my dead father again
or a voice into the future?

The telephone tells me that
I have missed messages.

2.

Sometimes what we thought was song
is a warning;

not that there are armies here
not that anyone believes in angels
not that the old riot as they rot
not that the farmyard slaughter
will contaminate us all
not that the blind cannot see
not that all cathedrals should become museums
not that every word we write has already been.

3.

They hold up their hands
to the light and the light
does not see them
and does not reach them
but the dagger
will do it

4.

The beautiful intuitions arrive when we are
about to be released from a dream or when
a voice enters an orchard
or when ten boys move across the field in Bedfordshire
killing each rabbit to stop the blinding pain and earn sixpence
a tail and wonder if God knows.

WHEN SHE GAVE UP THE MUSIC

When she gave up the music
I thought of fields in Somerset
when the light was voices and
the weave of seasons was in stone and trees
and the distant coast of Wales signalled;
and there was a church where there had been a false messiah
and a place where a horse had died and the voices of
pilgrims and hunters and the very lonely who spent Christmas
morning away from carols and bells; and the sound of water never
left between white grass and the lace of lichen and wind haul and
further down the coast a place where lepers had made light out of
silence and even the cows approached us as if we had urgent messages
but she had given up the music and the words were dragonflies now.

When she gave up the music
I thought of our Quaker ancestor
who said the piano had to go
and the three men who found that removing it was like
taking a wind out of the woods or birds out of the horizon,
the room left in a sudden silence, as if words had been unspoken;
I thought of a woman at her lacemaking who came to the moment
when a sale was to be made and the price was discussed and whilst she
found a way to parcel the purchase all the time she heard the voice of her
mother and saw the sun on her face even when for days it rained
or the children were ill and the lace that came out of these nettle days
and how she once said that she would be doing this when gates were gone
and pathways lost and the smallest creatures survived only in poems.

When she gave up the music
she searched for silences that had always been there and found
them in trees, in her garden and in the public park and in the grounds
of the large country houses where she avoided the crowds by never

entering those hallways, those reception areas with massive stairways
designed to make you feel small and the stares of ancestors and warriors;
instead she looked out of each window through old glass
to see what they would have seen, the formal and the layering and then the
release, into wild and what they did not own and tame,
as if they knew what music was, the rage of silence,
the notations of already ancient trees; beyond the ha ha
the lull of cattle who did not care and people with no voices,
their stories and deceits and passions hidden in the wind.

When she gave up the music
she listened to glass and signposts and the remains of gates,
she listened to a box of her husbands ties, she lipread postmen
and cold callers, she threw away the everlasting hearing aid and
when she visited the zoo it was up to her what noises they made;
the sea was even more beautiful silent and rain and passing cars
and without the signal of their songs birds being so bright;
often she turned on the radio knowing that the music was there
and words and weather forecasts and short stories and that she did not have
to believe in any of it, the theory of it, the orthodoxy, its hope;
when she walked into a cathedral she was aware of the tremendous
noise of the windows and the small prayer books so calmly crackling
and the light that never stopped falling; its silver, its whiteness, its wings.

AND WHILST WE WERE DOING

for Beverly in June

1.

And whilst we were doing what we sense makes a meaning
to our days and the way we dream and what we might be
remembered for and the way we spent so many hours between
what the gardens said and the books hinted at and the poems
desired:

> he was drowning: the boy found the matches: she reached
> for the top shelf and found two dead babies in a box:

and now we know that if bees no longer exist and there is an end
to pollination we will all be dead and there will be others on the planet
who may have created other gods and who may lie down with their
own fables of music and riddles and identities and screams:

> what he wanted did not exist: all of her life reaching out
> for something else: running away from the future: where's Jack?

Sometimes the god of things must wonder whether it is all worth it and
why animals, trees, babies, whispers, the way the human seeks for other
things and the delight of uncertainty sustaining wonder and poetry
and the notion of music:

> all that he remembered was gardens: the journey from Pembroke
> to Henley like driving through a film: who are we when we talk of
> the love of our lives and the sea the sea the sea never ceasing?

And then here we are again making the journey, the stones holding
sun and stars, rising along this avenue of voices and always believing
that is will be different, the dead birds will rise and the angels we have
observed will have different stories to tell, the sun like a barn
on fire and the truth of the matter hidden deeper than amens:

      we come with no offerings: we watch out for messages:
      the old clap hands: every day these candles and sometimes
      songs: about love and what did not happen and abidings.

2.

Sometimes when you arrive
nothing is as you expected
and then there are the walks
to places you know in your
hearts but can never reclaim.

We were at St Ewe where nothing happens;
between the war memorial and the pub it was
all about what had taken place so long ago and
who might buy the cottage for sale and the voices
that might be waiting in the rooms for new people.
What new people? Will they enter the church and
with what to say? Do they have a god and psalms?

We did not make it to Culbone because landslides
had stolen the way we knew; no small voices there,
no light between the trees where once the lepers had
left what might have been their messages, prayer prints..

When I looked down on Dunster there was a postman
and a dog and the sun collapsing on the castle; I did not
have time to search for the grave of Ann Craze this time;
I did not hear her long story; I did not visit her silences.

I would like to visit William Trevor and sit with him in his garden
and ask him about the stories that have so many silences and about
how not going anywhere may take a lifetime; about fields where you
may pass a man hurrying from one story to another; what is his name?
And about how every letter has a different voice and every window
is a journey.

PART 3

POEM BEGINNING WITH LAST LINES BY VERONICA FORREST-THOMSON

On the best battle fields no dead bodies
and our children have not been here,
that may come later;
and historians visit busily gathering flags and banners
and a man with a camera as big as Moses
and a librarian who searches between screams and curses
for lost letters and perhaps journals;
and here comes the priest again, hurling small tracts into the wind
that can never cease although words have no reason here,
all that has gone;
we are left with slow dawns and clouds gathering like low flying bards
and an American composer who keeps coming back in a taxi
to see what symphony he might compose
about the meaning of a battle, this way of death;
muffled drums for the old men who knew what this field might do,
bugles for husbands who tried to block out the sounds of their women,
oboes and whistles for the boys who had lied about their age
tasting stones in their mouths as they were felled:
what music can come of this, what sounds surpassing blood, what truths
in the trumpets and violins as bones explode and later, much later, bent
outlines moving across the evening sky searching for broken things?

THE BLUE PIANO AT MIDNIGHT

is about the hotel after hours and where all the people have gone
and the zoo when the war came here and what the animals said
and the bishops when they met in the marble halls between echoes and a
small woman danced for us when there was nothing but rain
and the poet who stood in the city square recited his sacred sonnets
as the wind and dreams and memory and promises stole us and we
all became ghosts and bits of string and every idea had a sacred hole
and a skinny man sat at the piano playing midnight tunes for always
and we thought if it is birds that will lead us to the pathway of eternity
let it be birds that we have never seen before from lost forests and nests
of ice and castles owned by crazy impresarios and recluse film stars at
the edges of being who feed their creatures from their own plates and talk
of their childhoods when everyone ate money and they could buy
the moon and how other children were kept away and gradually there
was a slow fade into rooms where there was only room for quiet light
and bird babble and the blue piano that finally learnt to play by itself.

BLUE ON BLUE

Not quite sure what happens now
because the beautiful dead keep answering
and as we walk towards October the old orchards
pull at the sky and the season begins to gently wrestle.
Our neighbour gives us berries which he loves and
apples that he hates and we both check our fences.
Some nights the stars surprise us.

Blue Wolf

Is not spoken about. Sometimes appears in the library
where explosions are taking place in the heart all the time.
Often appears in the church when the rush of messages
has been overtaken by organ music unless we are dealing
with death when the creature will hide inside a silence.
And then there is the story of the last man leaving the
pub needing to relieve himself in the field of snow, the
eye of the moon seeing him there, and silence broken,
and then the blue wolf approaching from the coppice.
The man jumps out of his skin leaving it on the ground
like a crumpled tracksuit. A figure in red racing away.

A Short History of Blue Dogs

There is no history; there is the temptation
and the terror but nothing written down. There
are some who will towards the end search behind
the pages of their lives seeking to understand. There
are those who deny at dinner tables and when speaking
to their solicitors. There are many who want to inform
their partners or priests or teachers but they seldom do.
Sometimes they see blue dogs in a painting or hear them
at the start of a song and it is organ music or jazz or a red
tie that winds them up again. And the museum has no
record of blue dogs and the family diaries tell you nothing
and there is no sight of them in family photographs and there
is no knowledge of a blue dog mural or mosaic and there are
no dogs at the mosque, the railway station, the old cinema, the
remains of the burnt down theatre, the ballet school, the hospital.
It is easy in dreams; blue dogs everywhere; blue dogs as the jazzman
hits the keys, blue dogs at The Ritz, blue dogs at night on the windy
building site and at the deserted airfield and a blue dog draped at the
end of the bed. Give me a Sumerian dog, a Dream Song dog, a rain dog,
a tangle of weeds dog just so long as it is the blue, the deep blue, the
shut down blue, the enormous blue, the kettle drum blue, the what comes
next hue of the blue, the shrapnel wound blue, the never before this blue,
the exploding parrot blue, the blue of the window that is not there in the
cathedral that does not exist where blue dogs wait for the man in the
blue suit, his blue voice, his blue whistle, his blue dance, his blue riddles.

THE BLUE DOGS OF ALBANIA

Blue dogs don't ask you things;
they come out from corners in a slow motion jog,
packs of them dodging in and out of shades and shadows
and things that have been, seeking the unexpected and hidden
and used, a ghost here and a buried thing there and things we
do not see that may have to do with small surrenders and loss.

They keep away from the boys who sometimes fly their kites
and the cruising cars near the cafes and the wrecked factories
and in the evening go down to the beach where wind keeps
turning over the pages of newspapers and the ocean drags
trash and sometimes there will be a well dressed couple who
are startled and start to run although the dogs ignore them.

Blue dogs sometimes sleep outside the library or beneath
blue trees, they have had their fill of cemeteries and car parks
and people don't leave things in the parks anymore. They keep
their heads down and get skinnier and remember the days of
big rats and open sewers and following an old drunk all the
way home in a street where the only light comes from mimosa.

In a Blue World

And in a blue world there will be other words
where to go into the silence of things brings a
plunge of recognition and the man with no poetry
is asked to speak up for us as we drown in drabness.
What is the colour of courage and justice and who is
it that we meet in dreams as our children dance in snow
and it is ghosts who tell us stories; again and again?
In a blue world the dancers will take us to places where
we no longer need words and toys are hidden in the long
grass and everything we knew has to be learnt again;
the name of each thing and what it has to do in being
and where each day is going. The gentle articulations
and the way that a song arrives in a garden of winter.

THE MIND OF BLUE

You do not negotiate with blue;
you either get it or you don't.
Blue apples have not been invented
and a woman in a blue dress is saying
something you don't really want to know
unless she is a nun and then you don't go
there anyway. Have you tried blue wine?
There are blue dogs and there is jazz and
as George Melly once said blue cheese is
far out when you have to sing. Have you seen
blue rain? It has a terrific influence on retired
bishops because it makes them think more
than they want to about the nuns of course.
Sometimes in winter the bellringers turn blue
and snow at dawn can appear that way when
there are no birds and the stars are still on
and the baker wakes up from a red dream.
The mind of blue creates beautiful birds and
butterflies and moths and the best blue of all
is the blue one that beat them all at marbles.

THE BLUE DOGS

Sometimes you can see the blue dogs
coming away from the mountains where
a man has been praying for four hundred years;
and you can tell from the way the pack moves
that they know about silence so deep
it is more like light in the mind and the words
have fallen away from shades of meaning
encountering the invisible.

BLUE DOGS AGAIN

This is where he came, escaping the past
and only seeking the fragrance of future
which would be this garden and the house
about to fall into the remains of a lake,
and the necessities of bread and wine
and whatever the visitors might bring
such as garlands or gossip and images
of decline and stories about the dead,
and whilst they were with him a few
might see the blue dogs that came here
each evening running across the terraces.

HORSE PRAYERS

Bosnia

After the hiding days, the silence days, the days when only
a tree might disguise and walking ghost tracks and streams
and the discovery of abandoned barns and sheds,

we could sometimes see, distant and as if in an old life,
horses, their slow movements, the way their deliberate motion
can be like wheat or wild grass drifting in winds.

It reminded us. It is as if all things can be transformed and
our current thoughts and words and dreams will become
a history and have new meaning and even mosaics.

There will also be the lies and denials and secrets
beneath earth and what the heart cannot forgive and men
who for the rest of their lives will go out into fields

to speak to their horses about horror. They will do this
in the evenings and when they cannot face their children
and perhaps when good news arrives from abroad.

They will tell the horses about some of these things,
looking them in the eyes, careful with the words and
the order of memory, as if approaching prayers.

They will tell about a woman who gave birth in a tree,
about soldiers who led an elephant out of the ruined zoo,
about the man who shot the man who shot his older brother;

they will tell about hearing the sounds of their village
and how the dreams were always about returning
and embracing and where was the money?

And the fields will become trusted again and the walls
be built of stories and the horses accept these accounts
and the older brother be present whenever we sit down to eat.

SLOW MUSIC

Albania

There is dancing, slow music, some songs;
many of them have not done this for years;
stories about the man have been dusted down
and his five brothers have been found and now
they gather here with the wine and cheese and
two brothers are dancing on the terrace, telling
each other tales, old secrets, where things had
to be hidden, not trusting some of the women,
in particular his wife who has lost everything
except for her husband's suit and a shirt and a
bright tie, all laid out by the side of the doorway,
all reminding them of a face and a voice and even
the man's hairstyle; and there are his shining shoes
and a single medal and a pile of the letters sent long
ago; anybody can read them but nobody does, they
cannot be sure what the letters might say and they
do not want to look the wife in the eye, admit things;
they do not want to talk about where some silver is
hidden and the bell to the church and the things that
they stole; they do not want to go through deceptions
and sudden loss of memory and the game of letting
the truth slip in and out like some lizard or insect,
the language of silences and cast down eyes; today is
about other things and showing some respect and how
deep the blood might go and dressing the dead man in
a suit and a shirt and a tie and shining shoes but no body.
Later, when the rain comes that evening it smells of earth
and dead birds. The mourners have all departed. In her head
she can hear them closing their doors again. She will never
sell his suit. At dawn she will carry it out of the house and
carefully fold its light as she buries it in the centre of silence.

THE WOMAN WHO WASHED HER HAIR IN THE ORCHARD

The woman who washed her hair in the orchard
did this so that the snipers could see her;
every two days or so, in the afternoon when
the light would stroke the back of her neck,
the water kissing her behind each ear,
the soap sliding down onto her shoulders,
her hands working at the shell shape of her hair
as she wound it tight, then released it,
then gathered it again, then let it fall in a swirl
as their sisters did, as they imagined their mothers
might once have done, as each one with a wife
could remember it, feel it, sense the motions of it
and imagine now a humming, a slight song,
the agility and performance so that they all
should witness, before the one who was drunk
let off his gun, broke the moment, ravaged this image
and it became her falling forward against a tree
and then the swing of her torso so that she faced them
for hardly seconds, for no reason at all, for them to see
her like some animal caught in a moment of betrayal;
and they were left saying her name, each man knowing
her name and that of her father and mother and the husband
who had died that winter when there was a lull in the war,
when he had become the lover again, the believer, bringing
in water and wood and talking of sunlight on the hill.

Heart Music

A barn door opening, whimper of a webbed window,
the way the wind walks through a field,
hush of a bough of owls,
and sometimes a figure far off dipping between hedges
that appears to come closer
and departing at the same time.

The music of our days and ways
as she moves her hand across the tablecloth,
as he carefully parks his bike,
as the dead tree catches hold of winter
as the window cleaner swipes light,
as the wild poppies pool across the lane,
as a stream that had vanished floods back,
as the washing line shirts hold hands.

Sometimes also it is the silences;
the single napkin ring,
the last days of the apple orchard,
the rain raising small stones,
the lost skipping song,
the shape of an antique spoon,
the old raincoat left hanging to suggest his presence,
the unanswered invitation,
what the thunder leaves behind.

Vanishing

Spreadeagled sunlight at the centre of the field;
a smashed tractor submerged where there had been
badgers; nettles, withers of white grass, strewn rags
and rabbit crap where the wind was always cornered.

And there they are again, the four boys, one of them
undressing, two as if on guard and the one who never
stops talking to the naked boy who is going to turn
himself inside out, from head to toe, and then return.

He has to keep talking to tell him what it looks like
from the outside of the inside out, speaking to where
the ears should be, making sure that the boy knows all
the time what state he has become in his undressing;

so that he knows when to stop, and begin to return, and
not get lost within the bone and strain of it, the other being,
the animal state, its blindness and necessities, its being beyond;
so that he can reverse what he has done and become the boy

again; the boy in the field in the sun again; the lookout boys
relaxing now and the one who did all the talking silenced by
marvel and wonder, the secret trick, the risk of it, forgetting
the man who told them how to do it, his yarn, his vanishing.

ASTONISHINGS

September is a good time for this;
they come out of the ground stuffed
with summer wheat and barley and sometimes
berries and bits of shell, butter shine and the silence
is like a stream of meteors as we lay them down gently
and do not want to tell those who will not believe.

Sometimes we are not quite sure what we have;
broken wings are normal but what have they done
to the beautiful legs and the music has gone cold
and the people who know about such things are
evidently terrified by what they now think they hear
which is actually another kind of silence.

The police arrive and they tape off the place
and the local media are told to shut it and a crowd
assembles in the inevitable rain that drips silver;
they call it news whereas it is older than words
and the God Men will invent extra silences which
they always do to enhance what cannot be said.

These things are what my father calls Astonishings;
moments when you enter future or as you run into the
orchard you see yourself in the nearest tree or when a
man walks through our village looking for a house that
is no longer; he should have been here years ago and
lived and died but he still has all this to do.

The Hail Mary Pass

The Hail Mary Pass is when God is out or asleep
and a very small boy has just fallen out of a tree
or your neighbours ask you to look after their dog
whilst they attend the final day of the Leg Shaver's Convention
and you know that for the rest of your life you will not be able to
resist thinking about the pair of them as they shave away and then
run a finger down the smoothness and inspect the shining baldness.
The Hail Mary Pass is when every tangent has been explored and
failure grins at you and the people who think you are brilliant are
actually preparing to clap their hands and you know, you know that
what you are about to do is fail, flip, fall, fade and you know that this
will be the end of life as you have known it so you come out with a
line that your mother used to crack when everything had been burnt
and before she had rushed out to hide it in the garden: "Well, there you
are you see", which cannot be answered, or even better "Tell Hitler's
sister", which I've just made up, or "I have to go and dig up my father
in law now because otherwise he gets very cold." All of which gets you
through the crisis and usually leads to other things, most of which are to
do with language games and sayings from foreign places such as "In
Georgia we have a house in every piano" or "Never keep a snowman
waiting." I mean, do they shave their legs in the same room or one after
the other and what about the ones who use wax? Or is that cheating or
like asking a man with a glass eye if he has a real eye in his dreams?
And the one that I like best of all and long to use is "And did God think
of it or did it think up God?" which has a shine and yet it is so lonely.

A Whistling Woman

A whistling woman does not let the trees
grow under her feet and knows the names
of the woods where each boy lies.

A whistling woman reaches for the tallest stories
and lets a silent room hide its secrets
even when the sun sits down.

A whistling woman will tell you about islands
in the mind where the noise of the geese
tells the farmers to close their fields

and where the man comes each day to tell them
that they have no letters or parcels to receive
and that the wind has their words.

A whistling woman lays out a meal each evening
and as she pours a glass of milk she says
the same name over and over and over

as if she were composing a sonnet.

THE RED PIANO

The red piano was last seen before the fields fell
and every tree was banished and men were seen
hiding the river in the church;

we had given them our language and changed our names
and if there had been more horses we might
all have escaped;

so twelve of us are left in this place without a name
and we occupy invisible places in our heads
and pretend to drink wine;

and once in a while something happens that is a gift
and we hear the red piano again
saying something very simple to us

and we begin talking about what it was like
before we were born
and what we will do

when birds return.

HAND TAPS OF A BRIEF ENCOUNTER WITH THIS TIME

for J G Ballard

Terribly sad. Hand taps. If we have you tap twice. Not that we may
hold you. But found. After these years. Perhaps thousands. The sound.
The colour. Bent texts and tribal.

When we awoke you what pain? Or was it more like millions of music
and benting and the earthing and the fire?
What did they put you to and the gods? Dance. Idea tree. And the
silences that were buried with you. You tribe.

What is this now to you? Our voices and the whiteness of lights and
the places where we hurt? We peace. We words. We welcome. We
long undoing. In the flash of sudden. In the sweep of incident. In the
finding.

Place. Now place. Now condition. Not another dream of another death
of another life. Not that village. Not that dance and fire and song and
blade of being. Not field. Not mountain. Not mother feathers.

How is it? The milk silence. The egg. The almost grass. Hoop. The way
we cannot be. The no.

The past loss. The tree silence. The seconds of us. The sound say.
What was never. Ever now. And how the millions of us? How the way?
This ends in seconds. Time slip. Knowing a dream. Past into future into
what never. Sounding. Something out. Something catching here. Tap
twice if you are there in the nowhere here. Tap twice if you mean. Were
there. Here. Tap.

Supposing. You cannot stay. Tribal. We cloak you in an idea. We were
silenced. No father feathers. Something like drum. Some soundings.
Noise as a voice as a way of being when we want meaning. Pulse. Red.

Memory makes bad loss. Whispers make bad beginnings. What is door?
What window means. We meet without language. Only what
is known is real. Tap if you do not mean. Tap if you about to leave.

Pulse red. Pulse blue. Where have we been? Here is some music.
Here are some colours. Terribly lonely. See the baby smile.

Please tap.

Five Hundred People are Writing the Same Poem

Five hundred people are writing the same poem
between rain and the sting of remembering.
They are sitting in cafes and sheds and beds
and at desks and in offices when they might
be attempting other things such as love letters
and complaints and proposals that might change
their lives and some of them are surprised that
it is a poem emerging because they had a short
story in their hearts and here is this poem without
ceremony and permission and an idea that keeps
unravelling as if it were a blue rose or something
more like glass blowing in the mind. And as the
poem begins to find its shape the five hundred
are hungry, tired, angry, sullen, uncertain because
they have never written about dead clowns before
or worried about an unfinished cathedral and what
is this voice and why is it speaking to them now?
Perhaps it will all fall to pieces, blow away, fail
because they really are not poets; they make love,
music, wine, dresses, shoes, jokes. They make meaning
to their lives that does not ask so much and is about
answers and not these broken prayers, retreats and
conversations in heart places and often empty rooms.

MIGRATIONS

for Tomaž, his words

Tomaž Šalamun is sitting in the beginnings of a poem:
it is a wheelbarrow, it is a tree,
it is about migrating geese beneath the moon,
it is about the silences of elephants;
it is about nothing.

Tomaž Šalamun waits for the step up of words,
the rattle of the secret priests,
a bat to fly out from the fat ladies hat,
the hum of the nuns as they swing in the park,
the idea of a cathedral screaming.

What these words might do as they settle across the page:
the boy and his kite rising into a grass sky,
the doctor who knows that the foetus is an angel,
the midnight lilies shining like shy girls at a dance,
the idea of the music propelling like gondoliers.

What the words will do to us,
these necessary migrations and secret births,
these flights above the mind that have their own calls
as what we have known transforms yet again, as we read
newspapers and the radio voice tells us it is all about time.

Tomaž Šalamun would like to hear the first words
as the café opens, the library wakes up, the sun runs into
the classroom, dogs hunt in the ruins of the cinema, the flower
seller is reduced to a whimper by a mosaic of roses: now
he reads what he has written: Lick Kafka, until he becomes kind.

WHEN CHARLOTTE MEW VISITS THE ZOO

It is the propensity of colour, what shades suggest,
the deepness of jungles and ravines
that are not here,
each animal lying down in places we do not see
that amuses her, these other worlds,
as the large birds stroll slowly
as the shadows thrown down by elephants make maps
as the ant eater totally ignores the human eyes
as each lion slumbers in a circle of gold
and the penguins scamper like nuns who are missing something
as the vulture appears to be devising a wonder or a war
as the wisdom of things closes in on the face of a young owl,
its not quite being here yet, its silence and slight fidget
as it waits for moments of awareness, discovery of being here.

But when it rains, when the sky comes down, when each cage
and shed become the edge, when we do not come out,
when we stay where we are in case things happen,
when the creatures might be beasts and what was wonder
plunges so deep we cannot go, when all that is shut in turns
on us and exhibits us and our children have become another
place, when the words that came to tell us things are no better
than the shadows of sounds, when the mirror drops darkness
and the money is not there to make things wonderful,
we do not, we do not do, we do not go out anymore,
the window does not do what it is meant to and when
I look for the roses; they have all been taken out.
What happens to the space left by the cedar?
What animals are here and tell me why?

THE END OF THE WORLD TAXI

It takes us there long after we were there.
We never see the driver's face and no money is exchanged.
The windows are always curtained with someone's mud and blood
and the screams they hurl at us belong to children who have no dances.
What is this place? Does it have a name? Why did they build this road
between trashed forests and dead rivers and joined up bends?
The taxi smells of denials and fingernails and ink.
Sometimes an astonished face flashes or we are held up for hours
as white rats are checked at the border and a soldier waits for bribes.
Sometimes a priest wants to sell us bread or a baby in a sack.
Months later in the hotel, at the airport, on the plane, we notice how
other travellers look away. They do not want to hear our stories.
They do not want to see our photographs or notebooks.
We sit in silence and think of home and realise that we are ghosts.

RED MOON, RED SUN

Sometimes what we were told as children comes to pass;
there is an angel in the barn, geese fly backwards,
behind ever mirror there is an alphabet,
the silent woods are screaming,
every bell has its god,
every night the books in the library read to each other.

What must we do to discover the truth?

In the concentration camp, very small, hardly on the map,
away from the cameras and the poets,
there was one day when the inmates all said
we will walk towards the wire and keep walking and whatever
they do it is what we say in our souls that will be remembered.

But nobody has ever heard of this.

Places in the World Where
There Has Never Been a Miracle

When we take down the stained glass window at the blue cathedral
each person holds each piece of glass as the sun runs out of it.

We are taking down the window in case of terror, the flames and
those who will hurl stones and urinate on every saint and ray.

Somebody holds the left eye of a saint. Another has a fish and another
an angel and I am holding an image of the infant Christ.

Nobody notices as I conceal it and later as I walk into the city
where the light is loud and everything heaves with words and music

At home I hide the infant Christ in a suitcase that has been to
every place in the world where there has never been a miracle.

When in a future time we are called to reassemble the window
I will return this piece of glass; by then Christ will be a young man.

I will find the place where the holy child lay and carry the section
of glass and fix it where the sun will find it. I have kept the nails.

MEN IN THE FOREST

They followed a path that they had known all their lives,
into the forest where a different language was used
and they were given other names.
When they returned nobody spoke for weeks, months even;
there were no songs, there was no dancing
and Peter had given up his whistling.
The classroom became empty skirts and shirts
and only when the pig gave birth
did we look each other in the eye
and offered biscuits;
and some of the men remembered the odour of beer
and we sawed off the chains to our front gates
hurling them into the lake
until the fish complained;
and we all went hunting for the hidden children.

THIS IS THE POEM THAT WILL NEVER BE FINISHED

This is a poem that will never be finished;
it is about a man sitting in the forest with a blue horse,
it is about my grandfather saying listen to the silences,
it is about entering when others are coming away,
it is about how we would like to arrange the dreams,
it is about the heron in the water in the image of sea,
it is about how some of them hid the cathedral bells,
it is about the woman in her garden with a red violin,
it is about what the letter wanted to say before it was torn,
it is about the way she folds the shirt for him to die in,
it is about remembering to forgive what is remembered,
it is about the three nuns playing football in Tirana,
it is about discovering where my mother hid her sorrows,
it is about the school bell when all the children have fled,
it is about the tremble of uncertainty when one is certain,
it is about what we were meaning to discover in the dance,
it is about the poem that we know will never be finished.